JOURNEYMAN
THE STORY OF NHL RIGHT WINGER
JAMIE LEACH

JOURNEY MAN

THE STORY OF
NHL RIGHT WINGER
JAMIE
LEACH

Anna Rosner
FOREWORD BY REGGIE LEACH

yellow dog

Yellow Dog
(an imprint of Great Plains Publications)
1173 Wolseley Avenue
Winnipeg, MB R3G 1H1
www.greatplains.mb.ca

Great Plains Publications gratefully acknowledges the financial support provided for its publishing program by the Government of Canada through the Canada Book Fund; the Canada Council for the Arts; the Province of Manitoba through the Book Publishing Tax Credit and the Book Publisher Marketing Assistance Program; and the Manitoba Arts Council.

Design & Typography by Relish New Brand Experience
Printed in Canada by Friesens

Library and Archives Canada Cataloguing in Publication

Title: Journeyman : the story of NHL right winger Jamie Leach /
   by Anna Rosner.
Names: Rosner, Anna, 1972- author.
Identifiers: Canadiana (print) 20200279807 | Canadiana (ebook)
   20200283979 | ISBN 9781773370545 (softcover) | ISBN 9781773370552
   (ebook)
Subjects: LCSH: Leach, Jamie, 1969-—Juvenile literature. | LCSH:
   Hockey players—Canada—Biography—Juvenile literature. | CSH:
   Native hockey players—Canada—Biography—Juvenile literature. |
   LCGFT: Biographies.
Classification: LCC GV848.5.L43 R67 2020 | DDC j796.962092—dc23

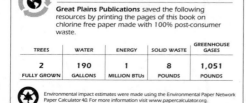

ENVIRONMENTAL BENEFITS STATEMENT

Great Plains Publications saved the following resources by printing the pages of this book on chlorine free paper made with 100% post-consumer waste.

TREES	WATER	ENERGY	SOLID WASTE	GREENHOUSE GASES
2	190	1	8	1,051
FULLY GROWN	GALLONS	MILLION BTUs	POUNDS	POUNDS

Environmental impact estimates were made using the Environmental Paper Network Paper Calculator 4.0. For more information visit www.papercalculator.org.

Canadä

FSC
www.fsc.org
MIX
Paper from
responsible sources
FSC® C016245

A NOTE FROM THE AUTHOR

As the director of the First Nations literacy project *Books with Wings*, I am always on the lookout for stories about hockey. *Books with Wings* sends brand-new books to students living on isolated reserves, the majority of which are in northern Manitoba. Students in the program request the types of books they want to receive, and stories about hockey are often number one on the list. As a result, I decided to search for a remarkable player and write a story myself.

It wasn't long before I spoke with Reggie Leach and learned about his son Jamie. I knew that Jamie's movie-star beginnings and his incredible story of unwavering perseverance had to be told.

Journeyman was born from numerous phone interviews over many years with some very, very patient people. Jamie and his mother, Isabel, revisited their lives and shared both personal and hockey memories with me, some almost 50 years old. Through their stories, I pieced together Jamie's life like a puzzle, poring over pages of notes and newspaper articles.

I admire everything about Jamie and his journey, and I know you will too.

FOREWORD BY REGGIE LEACH

There is no greater gift in life than seeing your children accomplish their dreams. I have been fortunate to see my son work hard to succeed and earn the highest honours in the sport of hockey. Jamie's name is engraved on the Stanley Cup, and he has also played on teams that won the Calder Cup in the American Hockey League and the Allan Cup in Canada. He has a fistful of championship rings. In fact, he reminds me that if he had played in the NHL as long as I had, he would probably have a few more rings to add to his collection!

Jamie, my daughter Brandie, and I have all played for Team Canada at one point in our lives. I wore #28 on my jersey when Canada won the hockey championship in 1976, and decades later, my children wore the same number. Brandie played lacrosse for Team Canada internationally and was recognized twice as Coach of the Year for US University Lacrosse. Jamie played for Team Canada at the World Junior hockey level, and he too received recognition for coaching the Manitoba Junior Hockey League.

Jamie and I are the only Indigenous father and son to have our names engraved on the iconic Stanley Cup. I am honoured to have the opportunity to work alongside him to share our knowledge with young hockey players who dream of playing in the big leagues. Jamie and I also play alumni hockey together. We even played against each other in the 2016 NHL Flyers v. Penguins Alumni Game. The game ended in a tie and we each got a point! We know first-hand that it takes hard work, focus and dedication to achieve your dreams. We look forward to the day when some of the players we have taught are also playing in the NHL or succeeding in whatever path they choose.

One thing I would like everyone who wants to play sports at a higher level to know is that, whether you realize it or not, many people will help you on your journey: your family, your community, your billet family, and your hockey family. You are never alone.

I am proud of you, Jamie, and of your journey. Love always, Dad.

COURTESY PITTSBURGH PENGUINS ARCHIVES

JOURNEYMAN

The Story of NHL
Right Winger Jamie Leach

A journeyman. That's what they call me.
I'm up and I'm down. Up is the NHL, and down
is everything else. And even when I'm up, wearing
my black and gold jersey, down is always there, waiting.
Whatever happens, this is my journey.

Chapter 1

THE RIVERTON RIFLE

When I was young, I came to understand that my father was famous. I remember feeling shy of the strangers who gathered around him, shaking his hand and holding out pens for autographs. My father was somebody who mattered.

I am the only son of NHL legend Reggie "The Rifle" Leach, though people often called him "The Chief." My Dad is Ojibwe, raised by his grandparents in a small town in Manitoba. There were only nine

Bobby Clarke and Reggie Leach celebrate a game-winning
goal in overtime against the Boston Bruins, 1976.

hundred people in Riverton in those days. My father lived in a tiny wooden house with no running water, surrounded by family who loved him. It was a happy childhood, though he did have his share of struggles. He had to learn to defend himself from the white kids in town, who used to pick fights and call him and his friends "dirty Indians." He dropped out of school after grade eight just to play hockey. He skated everywhere he could find ice: at the arena, on lakes and rivers, and on a little rink he built for himself in his backyard. It paid off in the end. He was drafted third overall in 1970 and skated his way onto one of the most successful NHL trios of all time: the Philadelphia Flyers' LCB line. Reggie Leach, Bobby Clarke, and Bill Barber made every goalie tremble in his skates. Both Bobby and Bill, or "Clarkie and Arnie," as my dad used to call them, were like family to me. The LCB line burned up the ice together. Tic tac toe, in goes the puck. The three lifted the Stanley Cup into the air in 1975. My father had 45 goals that year. Forty-five goals and 33 assists. Even today the best NHL players would envy those numbers.

People imagined I'd be like him, and I was, in some ways. Still, my journey to the NHL was a little different.

Chapter 2

GROWING UP WITH THE FLYERS

I learned how to skate when I was two years old, just after I had begun to walk. I'd wake up in the morning and ask my mother to lace my hockey skates right away. I'd wander around the house in a helmet, skates and guards, and a diaper. Sometimes my father would take me to hockey practice with the Boston Bruins, who swarmed around me like bees. He'd tighten the laces on my skates and help me onto the rink. "This is the big time, Jamie," he'd tell me. "Put two hands

Reggie and Jamie   COURTESY OF THE LEACH FAMILY

on the stick. And keep your head up." His teammates
would smile at me and pass me pucks. "Good shot,"
they'd say, "you're a Leach all right." My dad used to
let me check him in the corners. I'd push him as hard
as I could, and he'd crash into the boards and crumple
on the ice, laughing. "You got me!" he'd yell, pretend-
ing to have trouble getting up. "You got me." I would
laugh too and try to pick him up. But my dad would
just lie there for a while, winking at me. "Look at you,
Jamie. What a hit."

My father was traded to the Philadelphia Flyers
when I was five years old, so we packed up our lives and

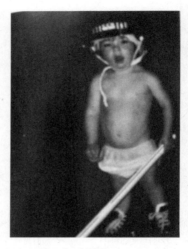

Jamie prepares for the NHL. COURTESY OF THE LEACH FAMILY

moved to New Jersey. We bought a house in Cherry Hill, a small town only twenty minutes drive from the Flyers' rink in Philadelphia. It was a colourful place: there were blossoms on every street in the spring and flowers in all the front yards. My father worked in the garden around our house, potting and pruning in an old pair of jeans. He liked the quiet; he said it gave him a kind of balance with life on the rink.

Our house in Cherry Hill was always filled with people. My dad loved to go onto the deck and barbecue hamburgers and hot dogs for us. He'd make too much on purpose so he could invite the boys over for dinner. "Jamie!" he'd yell. "How about we call Clarkie and Arnie so they can help us eat these burgers?" Clarkie and Arnie would usually show up with children in tow, a case of beer, and another package of hot dogs. Those were noisy nights, filled with laughter and mosquitoes. Sometimes my father drank too much with his friends, so my mother would take us inside to get ready for bed. I could still hear him laughing long after dark, or arguing with Clarkie about hockey. There was a lot of love in my house. Even if Clarkie and my father drove each other crazy, they were like brothers.

My dad travelled with the Flyers for weeks at a time, and I missed him. "I got a road trip, little buddy," he'd say, and throw me into the air with one swoop. He could carry me easily under one arm, or over his shoulder like a hockey bag. When he was away, I spent the days with my mother and my little sister Brandie, who was four years younger. Brandie was a strong kid. I had two pairs of boxing gloves that my parents had bought me, and I liked to pretend to spar with her. It made her laugh. She wanted gloves too, so I'd strap them on her little hands. They were so heavy she could barely lift her arms. I'd dance around her like Mohammed Ali.

When the summer after our move turned into autumn, I was scheduled to begin school. I wasn't happy about it. The night before kindergarten, I made a decision. It came to me while I was playing ball hockey on the driveway, listening to the sound of my stick strike the asphalt. I wandered into the house and found my mother in the kitchen. "Mom, I've made up my mind," I announced. "I'm not going to school tomorrow, or ever. I'm just going to play hockey, like Dad." She smiled and looked at me through my helmet cage. "You can do both. Daddy did both when he was little. Don't worry, honey. If you want to be a hockey player, you'll be a hockey player. I promise. But you have to go to school." I went back outside to think about it. I figured if I spoke to my father and told him my plans, he would understand better, but he didn't.

Everywhere we went, people were trying to catch a glimpse of my father. Sometimes neighbours we barely knew would ring the doorbell and ask for autographs. My mother would look at them suspiciously and say he

Jamie gets a helping hand from his father. COURTESY OF THE LEACH FAMILY

wasn't home, even if he was; she was protective of my dad. The family was once swarmed by a crowd of fans hoping to shake my father's hand at a carnival. "Stay close to me!" my mother yelled, fighting through the bodies. Kids from my school probably came over just to see him, but that didn't bother me. I was proud of him and proud to be his son.

When my father was home, he played ball hockey with us until bedtime. There were ten kids in my neighbourhood about the same age, so we had enough players for two full teams. We'd divide up the boys by the street they lived on: Pebble Lane vs. Orchid Lane.

We were ten kids playing our hearts out, t-shirts soaked with sweat, with only the setting sun as our score clock. We checked, spun, and yelled at the referee's bad calls. We'd argue about whether or not the puck went in the net, because it was too dark to see. At nightfall, mothers would start appearing on the street, calling us in. Sometimes they'd sit on the grass and watch, cheering us on, or yelling "CAR!" if someone happened to drive by. I organized an entire playoff series and crowds came out to watch us battle. Sticks slapped and crashed against the road. Once we even made enough noise to attract two curious police officers. "What's going on here?" they grinned.

"We're having our own NHL playoffs," I explained, trying to catch my breath. The officer nodded, went to the trunk of the cruiser and pulled out a few orange pylons. "We'll block off the street so you can play safely, okay?" Then they took off their hats and sat down on the grass to watch. We played well into the night, until my team was the last one standing. Kenny and I, we were a tough line to beat. Kenny was my best friend. He never really cared that I was Reggie Leach's son. He liked me for me.

Even inside the house, nobody ever sat still for long. Our house was filled with sports equipment; soccer balls and sawed-off hockey sticks of every length were scattered all over the floors. Brandie liked hockey too, so we played in the living room with my dad until we broke one of my mother's hand-painted vases. "That's it!" she yelled. "No more hockey upstairs! Down to the basement, all of you! Reggie, that means you. You're a bad influence." My father looked at me sideways. "Oops," he whispered. We kept our tournaments to the basement after that.

Even though my parents could afford to give us everything, they never wanted us to be spoiled. Sometimes my dad would remind me of his life growing up in Manitoba. "We never had much of anything," he'd tell me. "A small house, thirteen kids and no bathroom. I was hungry some nights. You and Brandie are lucky." My mother gave us lots of jobs around the home, but she always let us decide when we did them. "You choose," she would say. "If you play hockey now, you wash the dishes later. If you do the dishes now, you can play hockey later." That made me feel grown up. She was most proud of me when I took care of Brandie, or helped a friend, or stopped to make sure a teammate wasn't hurt on the ice. "I want you to be a good hockey player," she told me, "but even more, I want you to be a good person."

Chapter 3

MANITOBA

As the son of Reggie Leach, I was able to spend time in the Flyers' arena whenever I wanted. Everybody knew me: the players, the security guards, the janitors. My father would drive us to Philadelphia and let me skate on the rink alone while he suited up for practice in the Flyers' dressing room. Bobby Clarke always used to kick me off the ice when he got on for warm-up, so I'd go sit on the bench and watch. I loved the sound of it all: shouting, whistles, the echo of sticks crashing against the ice. When practice was over and Clarkie was out of sight, I'd go right back on the rink and start skating again. Sometimes I'd announce the game in my head, imagining that every seat in the arena was full and every shot in the net was a game-winning goal. As a kid on an NHL rink, shooting pucks, surrounded by some of the best players in the world, I knew I was doing something really special. Hockey fans everywhere would dream of doing what I did. In those moments on the Philadelphia Flyers' rink, I wasn't Reggie Leach's son anymore. I was an NHL star.

When he wasn't on the road, my father coached me as often as he could. He taught me everything he knew, encouraging me to be tough, to be disciplined. "Shoot to score, Jamie," he told me. "Shoot to score." He must have said it a thousand times. For him, if you weren't going to aim for perfection every time, there was simply no point in trying. Every shot had to be extraordinary.

I grew up with a stick in my hand, continuing to excel in every league: mites, squirts, peewee, bantam. I had a strong shot, good balance, and quick feet. With my father's help, it was easy for me to be the best. I felt confident on the ice, and a lot of that feeling came from my parents' belief in me. Still, they never hesitated to be tough if they felt I deserved it. My father got really angry at me once after a game. The coach had put me on defence, and I hated it. I was a forward and I wanted to shoot. I sulked the whole time, circling the ice and barely making an effort. "You've got to try," yelled my father, furious. "Who cares if you don't get what you want? If a coach puts you on defence, you play defence, you understand? When I was a kid, I joined the Riverton figure-skating club just to have more ice time. I would have done anything to play hockey like you do, to have the equipment you do." I sat silently in the back of the car and stared out the window, listening to my father's lecture for a good ten minutes. Every word he said stung because I knew he was right. I don't think I ever played that way again. From that moment, I always had a fire in me, practice or game.

For me, school was just an obstacle to hockey. During class I would daydream or draw pictures of NHL goalies on my desk. I only really loved gym. I was a good soccer player and an even better baseball player.

I became a catcher in Little League and later in the Babe Ruth league. Baseball and hockey were two different worlds. On the diamond, the pace was slower, more predictable; baseball gave you time to think about things. I liked controlling the plays and watching the dust come up around me when a player slid home. Baseball gave me a taste of what it meant to be really good at something. Even so, I was never as interested in baseball as I was in hockey. I always frustrated my coaches by missing practice. "You've got to be responsible, Jamie," one snapped. "We need you on the team. And if you can't practice with us because of hockey, then you're going to have to choose. What's it going to be? Hockey or baseball?"

I didn't think for more than a second. I just picked up my baseball bat and handed it to him. And I walked away.

When I was in junior high, I became a serious hockey player. I trained for hours every day, after school and weekends. The only thing I didn't like about hockey was dragging my heavy equipment around, so I started leaving it in the car. "Jamie!" my father would yell. "Come get your smelly gear out of the trunk and hang it up!" But more often than not, I left it there. Once, right before a big tryout, my dad drove to the airport for an away game with the Flyers and my hockey bag went with him. I had no skates and no helmet. I called my teammate Jimmy in a panic. "What size do you wear?" I asked, my heart pounding. His old skates were too small. I tried again, calling friends with older brothers, and finally found a used pair about two sizes too big. Jimmy and I each took a skate lace and pulled until our hands were sore. "Let's try pulling with our gloves on," he offered. But no matter how tightly we laced them, I could still feel my feet sliding. Even my stick was too long. "Let's go," Jimmy said. "You'll just do what you can." I was worn out, and it showed on the ice. I hobbled around the rink, missing passes and losing the puck to defensemen.

When I saw the team rosters a few days later, my heart fell. The words seemed almost unthinkable: B TEAM: JAMIE LEACH." It was the first time I hadn't been one of the best, and it hurt. Friends patted my shoulder in the dressing room, trying to console me, but I didn't want to hear it. I was Reggie Leach's son, and I was going to the NHL. My pride surged through me the minute I stepped on the ice for practice. I scored six, seven goals a game; I dominated as a forward and as a defenseman. The coaches just shook their heads. "What is this kid doing here?" Finally, they moved me up. I don't think I ever left my equipment in the car again.

My father loved a road trip. He was on the move from the age of sixteen, travelling wherever his hockey life carried him. Before he was drafted, he and Clarkie had played together in Manitoba for the Flin Flon Bombers. Together, they'd bought an old car for eighty dollars and drove it for miles, or as far as the gas would let them. My father wanted us to know Manitoba the way he had as a boy, so in the summertime, he drove us north. We had a cottage in Arnes, near his childhood home. There were only two hundred people in that town, maybe less. A few old churches, a cemetery scattered with withering flowers, and a restaurant or two, usually empty. Sometimes all you could hear was the wind in the trees. My father loved it up there; being near the water and forests meant a lot to him. When he was little, he used to run around in the woods with his siblings and friends, even after dark. Nobody ever bothered to tell them to come home.

My father surprised us by buying a camper one year. It was like a house on wheels, and Brandie and I loved it. If the Flyers didn't make the playoffs, my parents would take us out of school early. We'd pile into the camper for the long trip home to Manitoba, where both of my parents were from, stopping along the way to swim. Brandie and I looked forward to a big amusement park somewhere south of the Canadian border. My parents handed us long strips of tickets for the games so Brandie could win a stuffed toy. She was scared of the faster rides, but I wasn't afraid of anything. I'd point to the biggest roller coaster out there and my dad would just shrug his shoulders. "If you're game, Jamie, I'm game." We'd climb into the seats and scream as loud as we could on the drops. My father would grin with whatever teeth he had left; he'd lost a few on the ice already.

Our cottage was right on Lake Winnipeg, near my father's childhood home. I'd run out the screen door as fast as I could, full speed across the beach, and disappear into the water. "Jamie! You get back here and walk like a normal person," my mother would say. "The lake's not going anywhere." I played on the sand for hours and walked in the woods with Brandie to find wildflowers or to climb century-old trees. If any bark had fallen off a birch tree, my mother would pick it up and show us how to paint it or make a book. My parents allowed me to ride my bike alone, sometimes for miles at a time. There were almost no cars in Arnes. I'd just climb on my bike and wind my way along a road through the trees, and I wouldn't see another soul until I stopped to buy a popsicle at the local store. I'd sit near my bike, tracing pictures of goalies into the dirt.

If the day was calm, sometimes I'd make myself a sandwich and pull my canoe into the lake. I'd put on a life jacket and paddle out alone until the cottage was just a tiny spot among the spruce trees. I had a fishing pole and I'd sit for hours, silent, watching the water for perch. I always caught a few, but perch are so small, most of the time I'd have to throw them back. If I was lucky enough to catch a bigger one, I took it to my father. He showed me how to clean the fish and cook it over a fire for dinner.

Jamie sailing on Lake Winnipeg with a friend.
COURTESY OF THE LEACH FAMILY

The summer storms in Arnes came almost without warning. Black clouds rolled in from nowhere, and the wind would gust off the water. "Let's go," my mother would say, picking up beach chairs in one hand and Brandie in the other. "It's going to be a big one." I wasn't afraid of the thunder. The Ojibwe believe the sound is an *animikii*, a thunderbird, flapping its powerful wings to water the earth. The rain would come suddenly, fiercely, and it didn't fall downwards, it was driven horizontally onto the windows until they were

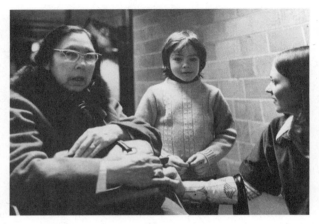

Jamie, his mother Isabel, and great-grandmother Kate in
the Philadelphia Flyers arena. COURTESY OF THE LEACH FAMILY

covered with a sheet of water, as though we were in a
boat at sea. The younger birch trees would bend under
the storm's weight. It could last an hour sometimes,
until whatever mighty spirit that had caused it decided
to move to the next town. I liked to listen to the silence
afterwards. I used to lie in my bed and watch the last
few raindrops trickle down the windowpane.

At night, some of my father's childhood friends
would visit, or his grandmother Kate, and we'd have
bonfires on the water. We gathered up every piece of

wood we could find until the fire roared so high that we had to step back from the heat. I loved to watch the flames disappear into the darkness. The lake became still, like a sheet of glass, and we could hear the cicadas and the night animals begin to come alive. In Manitoba, the land was so flat, I could see the night coming across the sky. The stars came out one by one over the water, and if we looked up after dark, we could see meteors falling. When the moon was full or the northern lights were out, my parents would wake us in the middle of the night and take us outside to the beach. "You just can't see this in New Jersey," my mother said, wrapping us up in a blanket to protect us from the mosquitoes. Blue and red flames would dance across the sky. Everything around me felt alive. In Ojibwe legends, everything has a spirit. Water, fire, trees, animals. Everything.

Chapter 4

TRAVELS: FROM DETROIT, TO SWEDEN, TO VANCOUVER

In the NHL, things can change overnight: a player can be injured, sent down to the minors, or traded to another team. Life stands still for a moment, and then you pack a bag and go wherever you have to go. When I was thirteen years old, my father signed a contract with the Detroit Red Wings. I watched him put a few belongings into the car, looking unsure of himself. He said he'd see me at the next game, where he'd be wearing a red and white jersey. And then he was gone. All those years as a Philadelphia Flyer were over in the blink of an eye. No more Clarkie and Arnie. Even though it meant leaving my friends, I was happy to follow my dad to Detroit, to begin again in a new place. I was never afraid of an adventure.

I began eighth grade at the local school and decided not to tell any of my new classmates who my father was. I wanted to be independent, to be myself rather than the son of an NHL superstar. I made friends easily; being good at sports helped me to be accepted quickly. No one knew my secret for weeks, until my teacher instructed us to stand up in class and tell everyone what our parents did for a living. I didn't want to tell the truth, but I wasn't a liar either. What could I possibly say? "My mom takes care of me and my little sister," I began, "and my dad plays hockey." Maybe the teacher would be satisfied with that.

"Really?" asked the teacher, looking intrigued. "What kind of hockey?" he asked.

The room went silent. "For Detroit."

The teacher raised his eyebrows. "Detroit? Like the Red Wings, Detroit?"

Jamie takes a powerful slapshot. COURTESY OF THE LEACH FAMILY

That was it. "Yes," I sighed.

The whole class erupted into screams, and I had to answer a hundred questions. In the end, I was happy they knew. For better or for worse, being Reggie Leach's son was a part of me, just as hockey was a part of me.

Because I'd arrived after the school year had begun, I missed the fall hockey tryouts in Detroit's Bantam league. I was offered a trial with the Triple A team, but after a tough skate, it was clear I wasn't strong enough to compete at that level. Disappointed, I settled for a spot on the Double A team. I discovered, however, that there was a big advantage to playing Double A hockey: the travel. I'd heard through the grapevine that the team was going to Europe to compete against other talented players our age. I walked into the dressing room one day to find it buzzing.

"What's happening in here?" I asked, throwing down my bag.

One of my teammates sat on the bench and began pulling on his skates. "You don't know? It's settled. We're going to Linköping, in Sweden. The whole team. We play six games against three different Swedish teams."

"Seriously?" I hadn't been to Europe yet.

"Yep," he said, lacing his skates, "this is the big time Leach. Are you ready?"

"Sweden," I said, shaking my head. "Wow."

A few months later I boarded a plane with my mother and fifteen noisy teammates. All the parents stayed in hotels, and my friends and I were hosted by Swedish families whose children were also our opponents on the rink. My family spoke English better than most, and I got along especially well with their son. We stayed up late at night, whispering about our favourite NHL players. On the ice, the competition was both fierce and friendly, but the Canadians had to adjust to the larger rink size. There was just so much space to move—too much—and little time for hitting. We'd soar full speed toward our opponent, always arriving a second too late; he'd see us coming and disappear halfway down the ice.

In the evenings, the players got together and wandered around town, admiring the colourful buildings and surrounding water. We stopped at a McDonald's, where we talked and laughed and ate familiar food. "McDonald's is good," said my Swedish roommate, "for other things too. Not just hamburgers. Good to meet Swedish girls." He wiped his mouth and winked. "Time to meet some girls, *ja*?"

"*Ja*," we laughed.

"Try this. Go to a girl and say, '*jag älskar dig*'." The Swedish players all nodded their heads solemnly.

We looked at him suspiciously. "What does it mean? Is it a swear word? Tell us the truth."

"It means 'you are beautiful'," he promised, looking serious.

My teammate figured whatever it really meant couldn't be too terrible, so he started up a conversation with some pretty girls just a few tables away. "We're Canadian. Hockey players." The girls nodded and said something in Swedish.

"*Jag älskar dig*," he told them, grinning back at us. To our surprise, they didn't hit him over the head.

"Oh, we love you too," they laughed.

The Swedes looked impressed.

When I arrived home from Europe, I was thrilled to be reunited with Brandie. My father, however, seemed distant and moody. It was harder to know what to expect from him. Most of the time, he was the father I loved, and then suddenly he'd be someone else, darker, angrier, not even a shadow of himself. My father had always been a drinker; it was common in the NHL at the time. All the Philadelphia Flyers and team coaches drank beer together at a local restaurant, surrounded by adoring fans. When the Red Wings missed the playoffs in 1983, my father realized he was nearing the end of his hockey career. To add to his heartbreak, his closest brother, my uncle Rudy, died tragically in

Manitoba that same winter. Rudy was only 36 years old. Devastated, my father's drinking worsened. He tried to drown whatever he couldn't fix inside him. Sometimes he even disappeared for a couple of days with no explanation. The Detroit coaches were frustrated, and so was my dad. He left the Red Wings and the NHL forever. He decided to play hockey in the minor leagues for the Montana Magic, thousands of miles away. He packed his equipment and left with a quick goodbye, while my mother, Brandie and I returned to New Jersey. I had to get used to a life without him. His absence only made me want to succeed even more, so I threw myself into hockey. I wanted to finish what he'd started, to be as good as he was, if not better. It was my way of keeping him close to me.

By the time I was fifteen, I could already see players who were destined for the NHL. I was beginning to feel the pressure. I knew I wasn't as physically strong as some of my teammates; until then, I'd relied on my height rather than my strength. I decided to intensify my workouts, spending an hour in the gym after practice. I became a powerful physical player, ready for the junior league. Late in the school year, my coach asked to see me before practice, and he was smiling. "I've got some news, Jamie," he started, "and you're going to like it." I had been chosen to play at the highest junior level for the New Westminster Bruins in Vancouver, where my father knew the coach. I couldn't even close my eyes that night. It's all beginning, I thought. It's all just beginning.

I was scheduled to fly to Vancouver in the summer of 1985. I must have packed four bags of hockey equipment. Brandie and my mother sat on my bed, folding t-shirts and jeans. It was just the three of us at home; my parents had separated during my father's year in Montana. He had left hockey entirely and rented a small apartment in Cherry Hill to be closer to us. I almost never saw him. I didn't know what he was feeling, what he wanted, or if he was thinking of me, living the life he had left behind.

"Maybe you'll need another button-down shirt?" my mother asked. "Or your suit and tie?"

"I'm going to a hockey arena, Mom, not a presidential dinner."

"Right," she laughed. "Don't mind me. I'm just nervous."

I fell onto the bed, looking around my half-empty room. "I think it's going to be okay." I told her.

"I *know* it's going to be okay," she answered. "This is what you want. You've been working for it for ten years already."

I got up and threw a couple of trophies into a bag, along with some family photos. There was one I loved of the cottage. I wanted to take something from home with me, a reminder of the family I'd be leaving behind.

On August 25th, my sixteenth birthday, I flew to Manitoba with my mother and Brandie, watching home disappear from the plane window. We spent a few sunny days at the cottage, and on my last night, I had a bonfire with friends on the beach. We talked until the last light disappeared, and when the fire died down, we fell asleep in blankets on the sand, listening to the water. My mother woke me at sunrise for breakfast. I packed up my bag and headed west to British Columbia, trying to settle my nerves on the flight. For the first time in my life, I was on my own.

Hockey journeys are filled with people who help you along the way. They carry you on their shoulders, and you never forget them. When you score your first NHL goal, they're all right there, raising your stick with you. In Vancouver, I billeted with a family I came to love as my own. Living with strangers seemed almost natural because my own family had always taken in young NHL rookies when I was a kid. My host family took care of me, cooked for me, and made sure I was behaving. I attended school for a few hours a day and worked hard to keep my grades up; my mother would only allow me to stay in Vancouver if I promised not to let my schoolwork slip. Afternoons were devoted to hours of hockey drills, intense workouts, and endless whistles and advice. If I wasn't too tired, I'd walk or bike along the oceanfront in the evenings, often thinking of home. My host mother, Evelyn, tried to keep me happy, and while I was grateful to her, I was still homesick for my family. I had lost contact with my father, and it weighed on me. There were so many things I wanted to tell him. I was angry with him too, for his drinking, and for his absence. I missed seeing him in the stands, grinning and nodding his head at me when I scored a goal. And I missed everything about my mother and sister. Brandie was only twelve. Since my father had left, I felt more protective of her. And now I was thousands of miles away.

If I was too quiet, Evelyn called my mother to tell her I needed to hear from her. I tried to steady my voice on the phone so my mother wouldn't worry. "Christmas will be here sooner than you know," she encouraged me. "It'll be wonderful to have the family all together. And by the way, how are your grades? I know it's hard to be away from class so much and do well, but remember, if you can't keep up, you're coming home. I'm serious, Jamie."

I could only smile. I'd heard the same line twenty times already. "My grades are fine, Mom, I promise you. I'll bring you my report card."

"Okay then," she laughed. "We'll see."

My visit to New Jersey over Christmas was bittersweet; my time with family and friends was short, and I wasn't ready to think about leaving them again. I reconnected with my hockey teammates and played a few games. I could feel the new strength and speed that had come from long hours of training in Vancouver.

I weaved easily through defensemen, spinning away from them, and found the back of the net with ease. "What have they been feeding you up there in Canada, Leach?" they asked, shaking their heads. My mother and I spoke briefly about my homesickness, but I wanted to be positive and so did she. I had chosen this path, this hockey life. We both knew there was nothing I wanted more than to play in the NHL. "This is the first step to your career," my mother said. "It's the first step, and it's going to be bumpy along the way. So we all need to be strong."

To make leaving home easier, my mother promised to visit me in Vancouver. She hugged me at the airport for a long time. "I'll call you soon with my arrival date in Vancouver," she promised. "See you in just a few months." The distance was the hardest; New Jersey to Vancouver was over five hours by air. After the season ended with the Westminster Bruins, I finished school and hoped to chase my dreams closer to home. I wanted to be a hockey player, but I needed the support of my family to do it. I needed my father. Without him, without all of them, the fire in me didn't burn as bright.

Chapter 5

THE NHL DRAFT

After my time in Vancouver, I celebrated my seventeenth birthday and headed east. I had been drafted by the Hamilton Steelhawks, a well-respected team in the Ontario Hockey League. Hamilton was a quiet industrial town, filled with factories and hamburger joints. It was also closer to home: only six hours drive from Cherry Hill. I loved my second adopted family as much as I had the first. We lived up on the Niagara escarpment, near a rocky cliff surrounded by miles of ancient maple and pine trees. Sometimes when the leaves were changing, we all hiked after dinner. The

The Niagara escarpment near Hamilton, Ontario.
PAULA BANKS. REPRINTED WITH PERMISSION.

family had a young son, Paul; we liked to watch hockey games together on television and yell at the bad calls.

My mother and Brandie drove up all the time to see me play, and my father managed to come to a few games too. Although I didn't know it at the time, while I was struggling with homesickness in Vancouver, my father had been fighting a battle of his own. After many weeks in rehab, he had quit drinking completely and was ready to face his family, determined to come back into our lives. Our first conversations were strained. Forgiveness came slowly for me, but it did come, especially when I began to understand that sobriety was his way of choosing us. Because my dad was still young, he thought briefly of returning to professional hockey himself, but he knew the pressure would be too much for him. He passed his NHL jersey to me and never looked back.

Having my father in my life balanced me, and I grew into a strong junior player. The goals started to pile up, and so did my confidence. Still, my coaches didn't think I'd be drafted into the NHL. "You're seventeen," they told me. "You're young. It'll likely happen next year, so be patient. But wear a suit to the draft, just in case. Never hurts to make a good impression." A teammate and friend of mine, Ron, was ready. Everyone was sure he'd be selected in the first or second round, along with my friend Jeff. "Come down to the draft pick, for fun," Ron persuaded me. "My whole family is going. We'll take Jeff too, make it a road trip. Camp for a few nights." I knew it would be hard to watch my friends be chosen before me, but I wanted to experience the draft. See things first hand for myself. We all piled into an old car and headed to Detroit, laughing like little kids along the way. No matter where I was playing, my teammates often became like brothers to me, almost from the first moment we shook hands. We understood one another completely; we all knew when to be silent and when to offer words of encouragement. And we all wanted the same thing.

At nightfall, we pitched our tents at a campground outside the city, watching its lights flicker in the distance. Thoughts of the draft kept us all awake well into the early morning. When sleep finally came, I dreamed of a wolf running through the forest. Wolves are fierce, proud, and respected in Ojibwe legends. Some believe that whatever happens to the wolf, will also happen to people.

My friends and I sat in the Joe Louis Arena with some of the greatest new talent in hockey, waiting for Ron and Jeff's names to be called. The arena was home to the Detroit Red Wings, and NHL victory pennants hung from the ceiling. I couldn't help but think of my father and his last year of professional hockey. Would my career begin in these very seats, where his had ended? When the Buffalo Sabres' managers took the stage to begin the draft, the crowd was electric. We all watched as players like Pierre Turgeon and Brendan

Shanahan were chosen first and second overall. One by one, young men stood up and began the walk towards their childhood dream. By the third round, forty-six players had already been selected. People were talking and laughing all around us, and a few proud parents were crying and hugging their sons. I had no family with me, just Ron and Jeff's friends, who had come to support them.

"*From the Hamilton Steelhawks...*" called the announcer. I realized Ron was about to be chosen: he was a strong centre. I reached out to shake his hand.

"Congratulations, buddy," I said. I was happy for him.

"...*the Pittsburgh Penguins select Jamie Leach,*" finished the announcer. Ron screamed and grabbed my shoulders. I stood up and put both arms in the air. There must have been applause, and congratulations. My father must have been laughing, wherever he was. We always thought I'd be a Philadelphia Flyer, but my destiny was to wear Pittsburgh black and gold. I walked towards the team manager in a daze, trying to put one foot in front of the other. He shook my hand and gave me a jersey. "Welcome to the Pittsburgh Penguins, Jamie. Hope to see you practising with the

COURTESY PITTSBURGH PENGUINS ARCHIVES

team later this summer." I wasn't allowed to keep it, but I pulled the jersey over my head anyway. I grinned towards the camera and a bulb flashed. The jersey felt just right. Like it was made for me. Suddenly, all my dreams had become black and gold.

Chapter 6

PLAYING FOR CANADA

In late summer 1987, just before my eighteenth birthday, I was invited to my first Penguins' training camp. I rented a small hotel room, threw my hockey equipment over my shoulder, and headed to the rink an hour early. I changed the radio station ten times, trying to calm the butterflies in my stomach. Years of training had brought me to this one moment. I had walked into hundreds of arenas in my hockey life, but this time, it was different. I couldn't help but think of my childhood watching the Flyers, of that little kid I used to be, cheering for my father and wondering if it would someday be me.

The Penguins' coaches welcomed me and showed me to the dressing room, where I had my own stall. A new black and gold jersey was hanging there, my name sewn on the back. I'd wanted number 27, the same number my father had worn, but a veteran player had already chosen it. I settled for 20. I ran my hands over the letters in my name. I loved everything about it, especially the way it smelled. When I turned around, I stood face to face with Mario Lemieux's jersey, which was hanging in his stall. He was the best hockey player in the world. In the previous season, Lemieux had scored 54 goals and made 53 assists. The numbers were almost unthinkable. I'd been close to hockey stars all my life because of my father, but at that moment, I was like a kid again.

It wasn't long before I became friendly with my new teammates. Paul Coffey walked over and introduced himself when I was sitting alone in the dressing room. He was an incredible player and new to the Penguins, like me. He'd averaged over 95 points a season in his years with the Edmonton Oilers. He was friendly and encouraging, telling me to be patient. "No one plays right away, so you've got to hang in," he said. "Rookies go up and down for while, until someone takes a chance on us, or someone gets injured. It'll happen." Then he hesitated. "I heard you play crib?" he asked. Cribbage was a card game I liked to play. "Someone told me you like crib," he continued. The two of us began to play cards whenever we had some downtime, or on road trips. It gave us a few minutes to think about something other than hockey. A coach would wander past us from time to time. "You two still playing that crazy game? How long's it been now…an hour? You're going to have to teach me."

When I wasn't playing cards with Coffey, I was usually reading a book. One of my teammates, Troy Loney, was a left winger with a wicked sense of humour. He loved to play tricks on us. I was suiting up for practice in the dressing room when he sat down beside me.

"How was your book?" he asked. "Any good?"

"I don't know," I answered. "To be honest, the ending was a little weird. I didn't really get it."

"Oh yeah? I wonder why," he laughed, holding a stack of papers in front of my nose. "Gotcha, Leacher!" he yelled.

It didn't take me more than a second to understand: Loney had torn out the last two chapters from my book. No wonder it had seemed so strange!

I chased him around the room half dressed for about ten minutes, but he was pretty fast on his feet, I have to admit.

As much as I loved being a Penguin, it wasn't long before I understood that in the months to come, I would be on the outside, playing an endless waiting game. There was just so much uncertainty, so many unknowns. I watched and listened, trying to find a way in. Most of all, I hoped. I needed to prove to the Penguins that they had made the right choice, and I needed to believe it myself. I couldn't make a mistake now. Not one.

After every Penguins training camp, I returned to the Hamilton Steelhawks, and later to the Niagara Falls Thunder. I was driven, obsessed almost. I didn't want to be one of those guys who was drafted but never actually saw an opposing team. The fear of disappearing, remembered only as Reggie Leach's son, was motivation enough. In the 1988-1989 season with the Thunder, I scored 45 goals in 58 games. It was hard for anyone in Ontario to compete with those numbers, and I was chosen to play on the Ontario Hockey League All-Star team. Still, I kept waiting for the call from the Penguins. Every time the phone rang, my heart leaped out of my chest.

In the fall of 1988, I did get a call, but it wasn't the one I'd expected. I was asked to play for Canada in the 1989 World Junior Hockey Championship tournament. It was an honour: Canada had always been a major force on international ice, and I wanted a chance to show the world I was ready for the NHL. The team flew to Anchorage, Alaska just before Christmas. About four hours into the flight, we flew over Manitoba. It had to be good luck. I closed my eyes and thought about my canoe on the lake.

We arrived in Alaska in the morning, but the sky was a deep indigo colour I'd only seen before on summer nights in Arnes. The sun appeared for only three hours in the afternoon, so if the team had an indoor practice then, we remained in darkness until the next day. We were all anxious to see the Soviets, or the "Red Army," as they were called. The year before, the Canadian team had beaten them in Moscow with the likes of Joe Sakic and Theo Fleury. All of the Soviet Union was humiliated by the loss. This year, the Soviets were out for blood, and they had the players to get it. We were all aware of the dangerous skills of their best line: Pavel Bure, Alexander Mogilny, and Sergei Fedorov. The first time we saw them in the arena, my teammates and I were silent. The Soviets wore red jerseys and never smiled, never looked at us, or spoke to anyone other than their coaches. They were followed everywhere by shadowy men. "They're Soviet agents," our coach told us, "here to prevent players from escaping to the US or Canada. Believe me, all the NHL scouts have eyes on the Russians." The Czech and Soviet players were all prisoners behind the Iron Curtain, forbidden to leave their countries. I wondered how many of them dreamed of the NHL.

The tournament was nine days long, and we were scheduled to play seven games. Our first two were easy wins against Norway and West Germany, and

I managed to get a few points. In our third match, Canada faced off against the US. The US game meant more to me than any other; it was going to be televised, and I knew my friends and family were all cheering for me at home. I couldn't sleep the night before. I hoped my wolf would come to me in my dreams, but I'm not even sure I closed my eyes.

In the first period, Canada dominated the game. I skated well and used my body for two or three good hits. Late in the second period, I intercepted a pass and managed to break away from the American defensemen. I started down the ice with my centreman right beside me, shouting. I faked a shot on net and passed the puck sideways, directly to the centre. The goalie didn't know where to look. I watched as the puck hit the top corner of the net and dropped behind the line. The referee blew his whistle and pointed downwards to signal the goal. I raised my arms and I looked straight into the camera; I wanted to make sure my friends and family saw me. The US fell to Canada 5-1.

The team celebrated briefly in the darkness, iced our aching legs, and then got right back on the rink for practice. We were still undefeated, but we had

yet to face the Swedes and the Czechs, both dangerous teams. We lost one and tied the other, while the
Soviets continued to destroy their opponents. They
beat Norway 10-0, and Finland 9-3. Rumours were
swirling about the Soviet team. Their training camp
was said to resemble prison, only with more food. If
we practised three hours a day, they practised six. The
Czechs were the only other team whose skill seemed
to come close to that of the Soviets. Though no one
admitted it, we were all just hoping not to lose too badly.

The Soviets were even better than we'd imagined.
It was hard just to get our sticks on the puck. They
danced around us, and we chased them like children.
Pavel Bure skated so fast he was almost a blur; we
could barely see the fluorescent green laces he wore
in his skates. We held on in the first period, using
every ounce of strength to shut their offense down. I
scored a fast goal at the buzzer, a lightning slapshot,
but after a brief huddle the referees decided the goal
was too late and wouldn't count. In the second period,
Team Canada began to fall apart. Mogilny had a
lethal wrist shot and scored three easy goals against
us; he skated through our defensemen like they were

ghosts. The bench was so gloomy, we barely spoke to one another. There was no sense in trying to find a weakness in their game. There just wasn't one. Final score: Soviets 7, Canada 2. The Soviets had won gold. We stood in silence and watched the team throw their sticks, gloves and helmets on the ice, then hoist their coach into the air.

The Soviet anthem played for what seemed like forever.

The 1989 Canadian Junior Hockey Team. Jamie is in the top row, third from the right. HOCKEY CANADA IMAGES. REPRINTED WITH PERMISSION

Chapter 7

BECOMING A PENGUIN

The 1989 Pittsburgh training camp was a turning point for me. I was twenty years old, skating with some of the greatest players in the league, and I began to learn from them. The minute I stepped on the ice, it was like electricity running through me. All I could think about was getting my stick on the puck and firing it past the goalie. Some days were more physical than others; I had aches everywhere from long hours spent on the ice and in the gym, trying to build mass.

I dragged weights across the rink to increase my leg strength. I did balance drills, stick-handling drills, puck protection and power turns. All of it. I was tall and wide, over 200 pounds, and the coaches liked that. My size helped me wrestle in the corners, unafraid to dig for the puck, and to push other players off me. Sometimes the coaches would talk to the press about my game, and I'd read about it in the Pittsburgh paper. "He's a strong player all around, Jamie Leach," they'd say. "Determined. Fights hard for the puck and stays with it. So time will tell."

At the end of camp, the Penguins held a team tournament. I got lucky; I was on Mario Lemieux's line. "Just position yourself in front and take my pass," he told me. "Then put the puck in the net. Simple." With Lemieux's lightning passes, I scored six goals, more than any other player on the team. Word was that the coaches were going to give me a spot on the bench; I was the team's most promising rookie.

During our last preseason game, I was in the opponent's corner with the puck and tried to break towards the net. Any player will tell you that corners are dangerous places. I got hit hard, and my leg struck the boards. I knew I was hurt. I shuffled off the ice, balancing on one skate and a teammate's shoulder. After a few x-rays, the team doctors confirmed that I had torn ligaments in my right knee. A little time to heal, they promised, and I'd be back on the ice. One month, maybe two. I was heartbroken; if my injury was serious enough to bench me, it could destroy my chances of a spot on the team.

I was summoned into the coach's office just a few days before the regular season began. I hobbled in, trying not to wince from the pain. The head coach sat at the desk with his arms folded. "I'm happy with your progress, Jamie," he began, "you know that. All the coaches are pleased with you. But I'm stacked right now with right wingers; I've got five. I want you to have the ice time you need, so we're sending you to the minors."

I nodded my head, trying to swallow the lump in my throat.

"This isn't a punishment," he promised. "It's the opposite. This is how it is in the beginning. I'm expecting you back here. Soon." I stood and shook his outstretched hand. "I'll see you then," I told him, trying to sound confident. But I felt I had lost the battle of my life.

I called my father. "Don't get discouraged, Jamie," he said. "I spent most of my first year in the minors, remember? And if I played in the NHL at all, my butt just warmed the bench."

It was true. My dad had been drafted by Boston in 1970, but with superstars like Bobby Orr and Phil Esposito on the team, he barely played. He only managed two goals in his first year.

"The timing of your injury is bad, sure," he continued, "but this thing is easy to fix. Rest a little, you'll be on skates again. Take it from me. I've been patched up a few times. I got holes in me," he laughed, "especially in my teeth."

The month in physiotherapy was one of the loneliest of my hockey career. The Penguins had all travelled west for a road trip, and I didn't know a soul in Pittsburgh. I limped around a hotel room, reading and watching television to escape from boredom. Five days a week therapists poked and prodded me while I fought with electrodes and machines of every kind to strengthen my knee. At night, I ran lengths in the shallow end of the hotel pool. After three weeks I could feel myself healing, and I felt a new sense of hope. It happens, I thought. We get hurt, they fix us up, and we begin again.

The moment I was declared fit to play, I packed my suitcase and headed for the minor leagues. I was going to be a Muskegon Lumberjack.

I just had to figure out where Muskegon was.

Chapter 8

MUSKEGON

It turned out Muskegon was a seven-hour drive from Pittsburgh, right on Lake Michigan. There couldn't have been more than twenty thousand people in that town, but it was beautiful. The beach had white sands that stretched for miles, so the locals biked and played volleyball in the summer. I rented another hotel room by myself, spending as little time as I could there. I liked to wander on the beach even after the fall winds began. I tried to clear my mind and just concentrate on the water. Still, the thought of fading into the minor leagues was never far away.

The first morning practice as a Lumberjack wasn't easy. I was still thinking about the NHL, about the thousands of shouting fans who all become a blur. The Muskegon rink smelled old and musty, and some of the boards were coming loose. It was nothing like the Penguins' arena, with all its flashing lights and jumbo screens and fancy dressing rooms. After a few games, I began to appreciate the team's skill, and the fans loved us. They banged on the glass and screamed and cursed from the first face-off to the final buzzer. We all fed off the excitement. The Lumberjacks were solid players, and they certainly had the fierceness of the Penguins. I began to realize that I was intimidating on the ice, especially in the corners; nobody wanted to take a hit from me. I pushed myself physically until I was desperate for a line change. I collapsed on the bench, breathless, and then stood up three minutes later to rush back onto the ice. I didn't want the fire in me to extinguish. I was going back up to the NHL, I could feel it.

I played fifteen games with the Lumberjacks and scored nine goals. "Leacher," said my teammate Glenn, "you're playing like you've got something to prove." I had barely settled into a routine when I got the call, just two months after my arrival in Muskegon. The

Penguins' coach was on the line. He was quick and to the point. "You ready for the NHL? Team's been floundering a little. Pack your bag."

And there it was. I was a Pittsburgh Penguin once again, headed for my first NHL game. I don't even think I said goodbye to any of my teammates. I just booked the first flight out.

The Penguins had lost three games in a row before my arrival, so the coaches were experimenting with new lines, hoping to change the team's chemistry. This was my chance to find a place in it all. In the dressing room, the team welcomed me and offered advice and encouragement. My hands shook as I laced my skates, more from excitement than fear. Somehow my legs carried me to the bench. I waited impatiently, heart pounding, until I felt the tap on the back. I exploded onto the ice. The pace was fast, much faster than in the minors. I tried to use my body to pressure opponents, but some of them were built like steel. In the second period, I passed the puck to Troy Loney, who launched it over the goalie's shoulder and into the net. An unstoppable shot. The five of us crashed into each other's arms to celebrate. There it was: an assist in my first NHL game.

I looked up from the bench, saw my name on the board, and grinned towards the box where I knew my parents were cheering me on. They had driven seven hours to see me suit up for the first time.

In the week that followed, the Penguins' wins began to pile up. The coaches were happy, and the atmosphere in the dressing room was improving. "Where've you been hiding, Leacher?" the boys asked, thumping my back. I felt like I belonged. A few games and another assist later, I got an early morning phone call from a friend.

"You awake?"

"Do I sound like it?" I groaned.

"Sorry. Don't you have to get up for practice any-way? Listen, there's an article in the Pittsburgh paper. Might want to take a look. Page C4."

I'd been interviewed briefly by the media after our last game. I rolled out of bed and went in search of a newspaper. The headline was even better than I'd hoped:

"Leach wings his way back to assist in Penguins' surge."

I smiled to myself. The Penguins were winning, and the world thought I had something to do with it.

Leach wings his way back to assist in Penguins' surge

By Bill Modoono

The Pittsburgh Press

When he left them early in training camp, they appeared destined for greatness. A team only a regular season away from a Stanley Cup, to hear people talk.

Since he rejoined them last week, they have been unbeatable, outscoring the opposition, 19-5. A team so impressive, even its backup goalie wins an award.

"I don't have any idea what was wrong," said winger Jamie Leach of the Penguins, a team that reversed an early-season funk with three victories that coincided with Leach's recall from Muskegon. "I've got nothing to compare how they're playing now with how they were before. But it looks like whatever was the problem has pretty much been resolved."

It also would appear Leach had little to do with the turnaround, although that is not an opinion shared by Coach Gene Ubriaco. The scoresheet says Leach had two assists in the three games, but Ubriaco thinks he has contributed more than that.

"I like the chemistry we have now," said Ubriaco.

The Penguins recalled right winger Leach and left winger Mark Kachowski the day before last Tuesday's game against the New York Rangers.

"It's always a plus when a team starts well when you first arrive," Leach said.

Leach is the son of Reggie Leach, the second-highest scoring right winger in Philadelphia Flyers history. Leach, who played on a Stanley Cup championship team in Philadelphia in 1975, scored 514 points in 606 games between 1974 and 1982. The Penguins hope his son will be equally productive, but realize that will not happen immediately.

"We've got about five right wings," said Ubriaco, who used Leach more extensively in his first two games than he did Saturday night against the New York Islanders. "Ice time will be a key for him."

That was the primary reason the Penguins sent Leach to Muskegon in training camp. Leach was impressive, but it did not appear he would get enough ice time to progress as he should.

"He needed some action," Ubriaco said. "Let him see what the business is all about. He's definitely made a move from camp."

Leach, 20, had nine goals and five assists in 15 games at Muskegon. Last season at Niagara Falls, he had 45 goals and 62 assists in 58 games.

"I was surprised they sent me down so soon into training camp, but it was the best thing for me. I'm in pretty good shape now and the time down there helped me."

Leach, who is 6-1, 200 pounds, is seen as having potential as a physical player, but not in the ways the word "physical" often is defined in the National Hockey League. "I'm not much of a fighter, but don't mind hitting," said Leach, who had no penalty minutes at Muskegon. "I like going into the corners and fighting for the puck."

"He looks like he could be a solid two-way player," Ubriaco said. "He's good for seven, eight hits a game. He patrols the boards real well and eventually he will score. That will come with confidence."

Leach was born in Winnipeg, Manitoba, but grew up in New Jersey while his father played for the Flyers. Although Penguins fans never have found much to like about the Flyers, the reverse was not true with Leach. "I didn't really pay any attention to the Penguins or any other team. I had no opinion of them. I just rooted for the Flyers."

Leach's father is busy with his landscaping business in Philadelphia, but father and son talk often on the phone. "When I was sent down, he told me to work hard and I'd be back.

"I've never thought much about being compared to him. I've always played my own game. Some people compare us and there are similar aspects to our games, but we're not identical."

Leach is not taking credit for the team's turnaround, but it will be to his advantage if the Penguins continue to play well.

"I like to stay with the same lineup when we're winning," Ubriaco said.

□ □ □

NOTES — Wendell Young, the Penguins' top goalie while Tom Barrasso is recovering from a hand injury, was named NHL player of the week for his victories against the Rangers, Quebec Nordiques and Islanders. Young, who had a 1.67 goals-against average and a .945 save percentage for the week, finished ahead of goalie Andy Moog of the Boston Bruins and center Wayne Gretzky of the Los Angeles Kings. The Dodge division of Chrysler Motors will donate $500 to the youth hockey organization of Young's choice ... Defenseman Zarley Zalapski and center Randy Gilhen skated with the team yesterday in practice at Mt Lebanon. They are a week or more away from returning to action ... Phil Bourque, scratched Saturday night because of a back spasm, skated yesterday and should be ready to return for tomorrow's game against the New Jersey Devils at the Civic Arena (7:35 p.m.).

Chapter 9

JOURNEYS

Like most rookies, I didn't see much ice time in my first NHL season. I watched my teammates from the press box, hoping for a chance. In the few games I did play, the best I could do was three assists. I was still unsure of myself. I didn't realize I was the same size as most of the players and probably a good twenty pounds heavier. I just couldn't find that feeling of being intimidating, of being powerful, that had helped me dominate my opponents in the minor leagues. It would take months before I really found my legs in the NHL.

"We'll be seeing you soon, Leacher," my team-mates promised. "Just one injury to a winger, and you're up again. Happens in a heartbeat. Everything does around here." I booked another flight and started the 1990 season in Muskegon.

The minors were harder to take the second time, though I was happy to see my old friends. I rented an apartment with my teammate Glenn Mulvenna, or "Mully," as we liked to call him. He'd been in the minors for years, playing the same waiting game as I was. His skates hadn't even seen an NHL rink yet. Glenn and I could say anything to each other, any-thing at all, and still know the other would always be there. He was family. We also both had the same midnight cravings for pizza and late-night talk shows.

One night Glenn surprised me. "Do you ever think about what you're going to do after?" he asked me.

"After?"

"After hockey. After the NHL. When we need to find a normal life."

"Not really," I told him. "For me, this is normal. It's the life I watched my father live."

Glenn laughed. "That doesn't mean it's *normal*. I think I might want to own a restaurant or something. Buy a McDonald's and eat burgers until I explode. Seriously though. You don't think about it? What comes next?"

It didn't take me more than a second to answer. "I don't have any plans. This is the plan. Whatever happens, I'll have no regrets. Although…"

"Yeah?"

"It would have been nice to be drafted by a team that didn't already have four other right wingers," I admitted.

Glenn sighed. "I hear you, buddy."

I made the best of those months in Muskegon, becoming faster and more precise. I began to visualize my shot striking the net before it left my stick. I didn't see the goalie; I only saw the space around him. I scored 33 goals in 43 games. With numbers like that, the Penguins' coaches had to take notice. In my mind, every single goal was one step closer to Pittsburgh. When I brought the Muskegon fans to their feet, their fists thundering on the glass, I imagined them wearing black and gold jerseys. The NHL was right in front of me. It wasn't about waiting for it to happen anymore; I just had to reach for it and take what was mine.

On March 5, 1991, after seven months in Muskegon, I was recalled to the Penguins. Glenn smiled from ear to ear when I told him. "It's about time," he said. "And Leacher, I don't want to see you back here. You hear me?"

"Don't take this personally," I grinned, "but I hope we never see each other again."

He laughed. "Maybe I'll come up to the NHL and see you first. You never know. Anything can happen around here."

It was true. Anything could happen.

A few weeks after my return, the Penguins were scheduled to play the Philadelphia Flyers. It was my first NHL game in my hometown, and all my family and friends from Cherry Hill had bought tickets. I decided to invite a few of my teammates over for a home-cooked meal. Knowing how much hockey players eat, my mother barbecued enough for an army. I asked the newest Pittsburgh rookie to come along: Jaromir Jágr, who eventually became one of the greatest NHL right wingers in history. He'd left Czechoslovakia freely after the fall of the Iron Curtain and had been drafted fifth overall. He was a dynamite player; the goals were just flying off his stick. His English was terrible though. The only thing he could do was nod his head and say "yes." My mother offered him hamburger after hamburger, grilled vegetables, salad, and he just smiled and nodded, "yes, yes." He looked pretty full, but then I realized he didn't want to refuse anything my mother had cooked. The boys and I started to have fun with him. "Yags," we said, because we'd already found him a nickname, "we'll help you with your English, okay?" I pointed to the salad. "Yags, look here. This is called *underpants*. You want some underpants?"

"Yes, *underpants*," he answered, his head bobbing. All the players smiled and nodded in agreement, and so did he, though he looked a little suspicious. My mother covered her mouth with her hands and laughed. "Don't listen to them, Jaromir. They're teasing you. They're making jokes."

"Yes, yes," said Jágr, smiling and holding out his plate, "more jokes. Thank you."

In 1990, the Penguins began what would be their very first Stanley Cup-winning season. We fought hard through the winter, climbing higher in the standings and gaining confidence. On March 12, 1991, the Penguins faced off against the Montréal Canadiens. Montréal's Patrick Roy was the most feared goalie in the NHL; we all knew what we were up against. By the second period, we were down 4-2. With just four minutes left, I found myself in the crease, so close to the goalie I could hear him breathing. I shot the puck hard and Roy blocked it, but he couldn't control the rebound. I looked down. The puck was on my stick. I didn't think. I shot, two, three, four times, until the back of the net rippled like water. The red light flashed and the fans came to their feet. My first NHL goal. I stood there in disbelief until I felt my teammates' bodies crowd around me, cheering. "That's how it's done, Leacher!" they yelled. Someone scooped up the puck and handed it to me. I could feel it in my glove as I skated by the bench, hitting my team's outstretched hands.

In the dressing room, the team congratulated me and banged on my helmet until it was so far down my nose I couldn't see. We were down 4-3 but still had another period to catch Montréal. Fuelled by the goal, I pushed myself as hard as I could. My teammate Kevin Stevens tied the game late in the third, ending it at 4-4. In those days, you could still tie.

When I walked out of the dressing room, reporters all gathered around me. Microphones were pushed into my face and camera lights blinded me. I loved every second of it. "It's a feeling you can't really describe, the first one," I told them. "That's what I was waiting for last year, but it didn't come. Maybe it wasn't a pretty goal or anything," I laughed, "but they all count. And by the way," I said, holding up the puck, "this is for my mom."

That night, I slept with the puck on my night table, waking every few hours just to look at it. When the clock finally showed 7 A.M., I wandered to the corner store in a coat and pyjamas, squinting in the morning sun. I bought an orange juice and a newspaper, opening both right in the store. There it was, in the sports section of the *Pittsburgh Post*:

"Leach hammers, gets first goal."

First of many, I told myself, first of many.

Leach hammers, gets first goal

By Shelly Anderson
Post-Gazette Sports Writer

Suddenly, Paul Stanton's rebound was on Jamie Leach's stick. The young Penguin right wing was parked at the bottom of the slot, staring down at one of the NHL's best goaltenders.

Leach shoveled the puck at the net. It glanced off Patrick Roy, the Montreal goalie, and boomeranged back to Leach.

"I took another shot. And another shot. It seemed like the last time I hit it, it just trickled in," Leach said.

Roy entered the game last night tied for the league lead in save percentage (.909), second in goals-against average (2.63) and tied for fifth in wins (23).

But under fire from Leach, Roy crouched just outside his crease, watched the puck slide off his right pad and into the net behind him.

"It wasn't a pretty goal or anything, but they all count," Leach said.

This one probably counted a little more than most. It brought the Penguins to within 4-3 with 4:12 left in the second period. Kevin Stevens scored 2:56 later to give the Penguins the come-from-behind, 4-4 tie.

More important to Leach, it was his first NHL goal.

He had three assists in 10 games with the Penguins last season, and was scoreless Sunday against the Islanders, his first game since being recalled last week from Muskegon of the International Hockey League.

"It's a feeling you can't really describe, the first one," Leach said. "That's what I was waiting for last year. I had 10 games here and it didn't come."

Leach, 21, might have had a chance to get that goal earlier if he hadn't torn ligaments in his left knee in the Penguins' final preseason game last September. A strong training camp had earned him consideration for sticking with the team when the season opened.

Instead, he waited for his knee to mend, then reported to Muskegon. Goals weren't a problem there.

Leach had 12 in his last 12 games. He had 55 points and led Muskegon in goals with 33 in just 43 games.

Which is why Penguin General Manager Craig Patrick, asked why Leach was recalled March 5, said, "Because he deserves to be here."

"It wasn't a pretty goal or anything, but they all count."
— Jamie Leach

The promotion was overshadowed by the Penguins' blockbuster trade the night before. Patrick sent John Cullen, Zarley Zalapski and Jeff Parker to Hartford, where GM Eddie Johnston was offering Ron Francis, Ulf Samuelsson and Grant Jennings.

It was Johnston, the former Penguin GM, who drafted Leach in the third round in 1987.

Between Johnston and Patrick came Tony Esposito. And there have been four different Penguin coaches while Leach has been in the organization.

"I feel like Eddie Johnston liked me a lot," Leach said. "Then they changed to Esposito and I wasn't sure what was going to happen, but he liked me a lot. Then Craig.

"It keeps changing. But I think I have a future here, although I think if the management can stay the same for a while, that will work in my favor."

One thing various Penguin officials have liked about Leach is his size — 6 feet 1, 207 pounds. And Leach said just because hockey rinks are rounded doesn't mean he can't find the corners and dig out the puck.

But he admits there have been times of frustration.

"[The Penguins] are stacked at right wing," he said.

After his recall, Leach sat for three games before a foot injury to Jiri Hrdina opened a spot. And in the third period of last night's tie, Leach played only one shift — in the first two minutes, when right wing Mark Recchi was in the penalty box.

"It gets a little disappointing," Leach said, of waiting to work his way into a regular spot. "You get down on yourself. But my family helps. They talk to me a lot, tell me to keep my hopes up and my chances will come."

That family includes his father, Reggie, who found himself a niche with the Philadelphia Flyers in the 1970s and helped them win two Stanley Cups.

Chapter 10

LOOKING BACK

I may not have been a legend like my father,
but I played professional hockey for over a decade,
and I'm proud of that. Being a journeyman helped
me meet friends and teammates all over the world.
All of them are family to me.

The years after my first NHL goal were filled with the ups and downs of a true journeyman. I had moments of triumph and moments I wish I could forget, including an elbow to the face that shattered my jaw and kept me sidelined during the 1992 Stanley Cup playoffs. Still, I

COURTESY PITTSBURGH PENGUINS ARCHIVES

wouldn't give up those years for anything in the world. None of it. Not the NHL trades, the trips down to the minors and back up again, or the moments I spent with my teammates, talking hockey, laughing, arguing even, and especially, hoping for the same dream. What I loved most about professional hockey was the brotherhood, the friends who all travelled with me throughout my teenage years and my twenties. Some of those players became the best the NHL had ever seen. Others never dressed for a single game. Those boys came and went, with no trophies, no glory, and no Stanley Cup. But I doubt they have regrets. They still gave it a shot, and if they hadn't, they always would have wondered.

I did finally live the moment I had dreamed of for so many years, but it too was a complicated journey. When the Pittsburgh Penguins raised the Stanley Cup in 1991, I was torn; I was thrilled to be on a championship team, but I hadn't seen enough ice time to have my name engraved on the Cup. The next season, though, everything changed in an instant, just as it always does in the NHL. In January of 1992, Jaromir Jágr was suspended for accidentally running into a referee, and I began to suit up regularly to replace him. I played thirty-eight games with the Penguins, managing five goals and four assists. The team was unstoppable.

On June 1, 1992, the Pittsburgh Penguins won the Stanley Cup championship for a second straight year, and this time, I had played a significant role. It's a victory I will never forget. I will never forget rushing onto the ice after the final buzzer in shoes and a shirt, broken jaw and all, and throwing my arms around coaches, players, and trainers. When someone handed me the Cup, I kissed it and hoisted it over my head. It was pure joy.

My name is engraved on the Cup above my father's, fifteen years apart. We're proud to be the only Indigenous father and son to win the Stanley Cup. We're united forever in sterling silver, and in our love for the game. And that's just how it should be.

AFTERWORD

After the 1991-92 season, Jamie continued his hockey journey, playing in the NHL for the Hartford Whalers (now the Carolina Hurricanes) and the Florida Panthers. He moved up, down, and sideways, from the minor leagues to the NHL, and then later played in Britain for the Nottingham Panthers. He won seven different championships all over the world. After his retirement in 2001, Jamie coached hockey and was awarded Coach of the Year in the Manitoba Junior Hockey League. He lives in Winnipeg with his wife, Shannon, and son, Jaxon.

Reggie "The Rifle" Leach had an outstanding NHL career, making his unforgettable mark in history with the Philadelphia Flyers from 1974-1982.

Jamie and Reggie holding a hockey workshop for First Nations youth in Nunavut, 2015. KELCEY WRIGHT. REPRINTED WITH PERMISSION

Fuelled by the talents of Reggie Leach, Bobby Clarke, and Bill Barber, the Flyers won the Stanley Cup championship in 1975. In 1976, the Philadelphia Flyers were unable to repeat their Stanley Cup win against the Montréal Canadiens. Despite the loss, Reggie scored a record 19 goals during the playoffs, becoming the first member of a defeated team to win the prestigious Conn Smythe Trophy.

In 2006, Jamie and Reggie Leach founded the Winnipeg-based hockey school Shoot to Score. The program travels to isolated First Nations communities in the far north to help children improve their

Reggie, Jamie, Jamie's nephew Hunter and son Jaxon
(in white). The wolf on the Shoot to Score jersey
is Jamie's spirit guide. COURTESY OF THE LEACH FAMILY

hockey skills, on and off the ice. Reggie also acts as a life coach, discussing his own past struggles with alcoholism, which he conquered over thirty years ago. In 2015, Reggie released his own biography, *The Riverton Rifle: My Story—Straight Shooting on Hockey and on Life.*

Jamie and Reggie's tenacious spirits and generous hearts are an inspiration to people everywhere.